Pterodactyl

BY BARBARA ALPERT

AMICUS HIGH INTEREST ❖ AMICUS INK

Amicus High Interest and Amicus Ink are imprints of Amicus
P.O. Box 1329, Mankato, MN 56002
www.amicuspublishing.us

Library of Congress Cataloging-in-Publication Data
Alpert, Barbara.
 Pterodactyl / by Barbara Alpert.
    pages cm. -- (Digging for dinosaurs)
 Audience: K to grade 3.
 Summary: "Describes how the Pterodactyl and other
pterosaurs were discovered, how paleontologists study their
bones, and what the fossil evidence tells us about these
ancient flying lizards"-- Provided by publisher.
 Includes bibliographical references and index.
 ISBN 978-1-60753-366-5 (library binding)
 ISBN 978-1-60753-414-3 (ebook)
 ISBN 978-1-68152-054-4 (paperback)
 1. Pterodactyls--Juvenile literature. 2. Paleontology--Juvenile
literature. I. Title.
 QE862.P7A47 2014
 567.918--dc23
                        2012036066

Photo Credits
Dreamstime, cover; Shutterstock Images, 5; Spencer Sutton/
Getty Images, 7; Georgios Kollidas/Shutterstock Images, 8;
John Cancalosi/Getty Images, 11; SuperStock, 12; Dorling
Kindersley RF/Thinkstock, 15, 16; Getty Images, 19; Universal
Images Group/SuperStock, 20; Mark P. Witton/Science
Source, 23; Mariano Izquierdo/La Nacion/AP Images, 24,
27; Kevork Djansezian/Getty Images, 28

Editor   Rebecca Glaser
Series Designer   Kathleen Petelinsek
Page Production   Red Line Editorial, Inc.

Printed in the United States of America at Corporate Graphics
in North Mankato, Minnesota.
3-2015 / P.O. 1245

HC 10 9 8 7 6 5 4
PB 10 9 8 7 6 5 4 3 2 1

Table of Contents

What is a Pterodactyl?

It's a bird! It's a bat! No, it's a flying **lizard**
swooping across the sky! The Pterodactyl
lived in the time of dinosaurs. Its wings
let it fly high over water and land. Its large
eyes helped it spot food from far away.

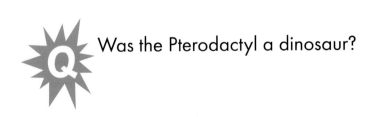 Was the Pterodactyl a dinosaur?

Two flying lizards soar above a canyon.

 No. All dinosaurs lived on land and did not fly. A Pterodactyl was a flying **reptile**.

What did this large flying animal look like? Pterodactyl had four fingers. Three short ones had claws. The fourth finger was very long and attached to its wings. The wings had no feathers. They were made of thin skin. Pterodactyl had a jaw filled with small sharp teeth. It ate fish and small animals.

The Pterodactyl was a reptile.
It had wings, but no feathers.

Scientist Georges Cuvier gave the Pterodactyl its name.

The Discovery of Pterodactyl

In 1784, a scientist was working in a German **quarry**. He was looking for **fossils**. One day he saw a skeleton with wings! He thought it was a sea animal. Later, the skeleton was sent to Georges Cuvier. He was a scientist in France. Cuvier said the fossil was a flying reptile. He named it Pterodactyl. The name means "winged finger."

More Pterodactyl fossils were found in Germany. Some were found in other parts of Europe. Scientists studied them. The wings could bend and curve. This let Pterodactyls fly faster in the wind. A Pterodactyl skull showed the size of its brain. It was big compared to the size of its body.

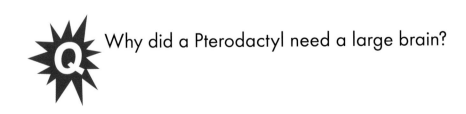 Why did a Pterodactyl need a large brain?

A Pterodactyl fossil
shows its large head.

 A large brain could control its wings. They also
had to be smart to not get lost while flying.

A group of Pteranodon hunt for fish with their toothless beaks.

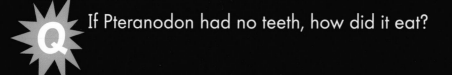

If Pteranodon had no teeth, how did it eat?

At first, Pterodactyls were found only in Europe. Then in 1870, a **paleontologist** named O.C. Marsh found one in Kansas. It had longer wings. Its bones were very light. He named it "western winged finger." A skull was found in 1876. It had no teeth. Marsh knew it was not the same. So he renamed it Pteranodon, or "wing without tooth."

Pteranodon ate like many birds. It grabbed fish and opened clams with its beak.

Other Winged Lizards

More fossils of flying lizards were dug up. They looked like Pteranodon and Pterodactyl. Scientists put all the winged lizards in a group called pterosaurs. They compared them. Pteranodon bones were much larger than those of the Pterodactyl.

The Pteranodon and Pterodactyl
are both pterosaurs.

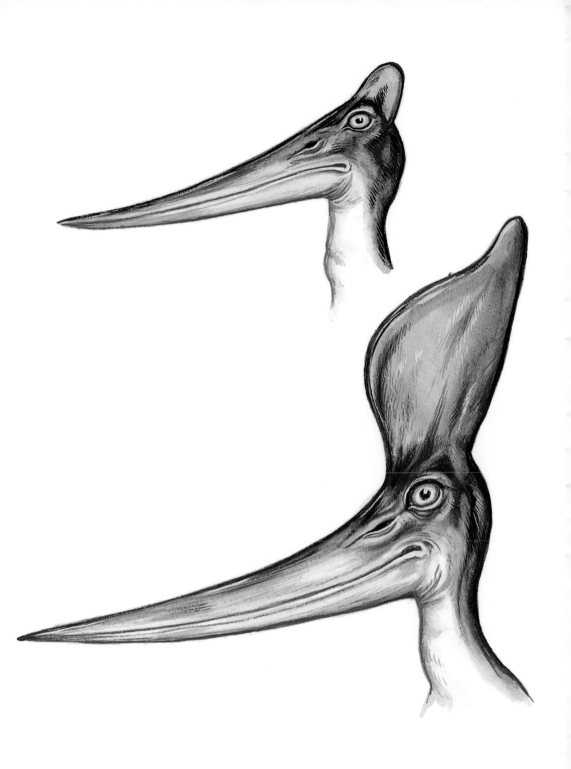

Each new fossil gave scientists more clues. Most winged lizards had a bony head **crest**. Some think the crest helped pterosaurs fly smoothly. Others said male pterosaurs used them to fight. Maybe the crest helped **attract** a female. No one knows for sure.

Most pterosaurs had bony head crests of different sizes.

In 1971, Douglas Lawson was in Big Bend National Park in Texas. He spotted a large bone sticking out of the ground. He dug it up. The bone was hollow. And it was 18 feet (5.5 m) long! It looked like part of a giant Pterodactyl. Lawson was a college student at the time. He and his professor, Dr. Wann Langston Jr., began looking for answers.

Paleontologists in Texas get fossils ready to transport.

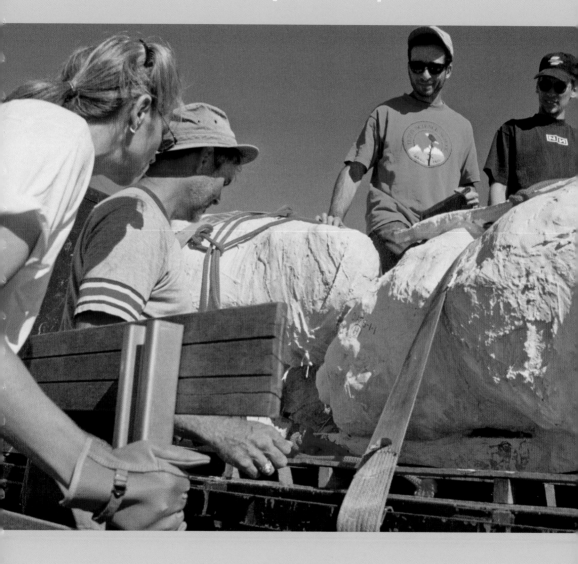

At one time, flying reptiles filled
the sky with their large wings.

Q Just how big was a Quetzalcoatlus?

Dr. Langston studied the long, hollow bone. He said it must be from a pterosaur wing. Lawson named his find Quetzalcoatlus, after a god of the Aztecs. Dr. Langston dug more nearby. He found more pterosaur fossils. They were not as big as Queztalcoatlus. But he found wing and body bones. He could study more of the animal.

 Its wingspan was 39 feet (15 m). It could cover a small car with one wing!

Fossil Clues to Study

Scientists did not know how Pterodactyl and its cousins had babies. Maybe they laid eggs. But there was no proof. Finally in 2004, three fossil pterosaur eggs were found! Two were found in China. One was found in Argentina. The eggs had soft, leathery shells like turtle or crocodile eggs. And they had fossils of baby pterosaurs inside!

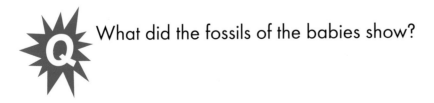 **Q** What did the fossils of the babies show?

Pterosaurs hatched from eggs.

 Baby pterosaurs grew fast. They could fly soon after birth.

In Argentina, the egg was found near many pterosaur bones. The bones were from pterosaurs of all ages. These fossils show that pterosaurs lived in groups. Scientists think they took care of their babies. The mothers may have buried their eggs. That would keep the eggs from drying out. It would also keep the eggs safe from dinosaurs.

Many dinosaur bones were found in Argentina.

China was home to many Pterodactyl
species. In 2008, a tiny skeleton was dug
up in China. It looked like a Pterodactyl.
But it had curved foot bones. That let it
perch in a tree. In 2009, scientists found
a new type of pterosaur. They named it
Darwinopterus. It had a long tail. In 2011,
they found a new fossil. It was a female
Darwinopterus with an egg!

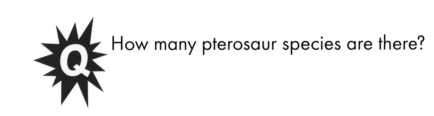 How many pterosaur species are there?

Scientists continue to discover dinosaur fossils in the ground.

A More than 100!

LEFT HUMERUS RADIUS and ULNA

28

Pterosaurs Today

You can see pterosaur bones in many museums. Scientists still study these flying lizards. Some now think they were like pelicans. Did they have a throat pouch to hold food for their babies? Scientists hope to find more pterosaur fossils. There is always more to learn!

Pterosaur fossils come in many shapes and sizes.

Glossary

attract To get the attention of someone or something.

crest A bone that sticks up on an animal's head.

fossil The remains of a plant or animal of a past age preserved in earth or rock.

lizard A reptile with a scaly body, four legs, and a long tail.

paleontologist A scientist who studies fossils.

quarry A place where stone is dug from the ground.

reptile Any of a group of vertebrate animals that breathe air (as snakes, lizards, turtles, and alligators) that usually lay eggs and have skin covered with scales or bony plates.

species A group of animals that have the same body features and can make babies together.

swooping Flying back and forth and up and down.

Read More

Lessem, Don. *National Geographic Kids Ultimate Dinopedia*. Washington, D.C.: National Geographic Children's Books, 2010.

Riggs, Kate. *Pterodactyls*. When Dinosaurs Lived. Mankato, Minn.: Creative Education, 2012.

Stauton, Joseph. *Dinosaurs in the Sky*. Discover the Dinosaurs. Mankato, Minn.: Amicus, 2011.

Websites

Dinosaurs for Kids – KidsDinos.com
http://www.kidsdinos.com/

Pterodactyl Facts – Kids Dig Dinos
http://www.kidsdigdinos.com/Dinosaurs/pterodactyl.htm

Pterodactyls – Enchanted Learning
http://www.enchantedlearning.com/subjects/dinosaurs/dinos/Pterodactyl.shtml

Queztalcoaltus—TheDinosaurs.org
http://www.thedinosaurs.org/dinosaurs/quetzalcoatlus.aspx

Index

About the Author

Barbara Alpert has written more than 20 children's books and many books for adults. She lives in New York City, where she works as an editor. She loves to travel and has collected fossils in New York, New Jersey, Montana, and Pennsylvania.